Ibi Lepscky

Marie Curie

Illustrated by Paolo Cardoni
Translated by Marcel Danesi, University of Toronto

Marie was shy, sensitive, emotional. She took everything quite seriously and she had a keen sense of justice.

When she thought something was unfair, she would cry suddenly.

She was the youngest of five.

Her mother had given each child a short, delightful nickname. Marie, who was the youngest, had more nicknames than the others: Manya, Manyusia, Manyusina, Anciupecio.

That last funny nickname was actually the first one her mother gave her, when Marie was still in the cradle.

Books were her favorite pastime.

She would sit on the carpet and leaf through a book, page after page, even though she barely knew how to speak and how to walk.

"That's strange," her mother told her father one day, "I've seen our Manyusia, Manyusina, Anciupecio leaf thoughtfully through any book whatsoever, even those without pictures!"

But then she thought, "Maybe she likes the rustle of the paper!"

Marie and her family lived in Warsaw, the capital of Poland.

Each morning, after her brothers and sisters had gone off to school, Marie would go around the house with the look of a lost child, and then tiptoe into the living room.

She found the living room to be a fascinating, stupendous place.

She liked everything about it: the tall bookcase crammed with books, the mahogany writing desk full of drawers,

the red velvet sofa, the bluish-gray clock, the precious cup
and saucer from France that no one was ever allowed to touch,
the table with a checkered marble top, and the barometer that
her father would carefully set and clean on certain specific
days.

But above all else she liked the glass cabinet that contained numerous small, mysterious objects. There were tiny glass tubes, miniature scales, strange and complicated instruments that were hard to figure out, and many strangely-colored rocks.

There were very dark ones with remarkable blue stripes. There were others that had small lumps in them, no doubt made of silver. There were transparent ones that resembled chunks of ice. There were very yellow ones. But Marie's favorite rock was a very beautiful pink one.

Marie never tired of admiring those enchanting objects. Each day she would discover something that she had not noticed before. She would have loved to touch them!

One day her father caught her in front of the cabinet.

"I see that you're admiring my physics equipment, Manyusia," he said smiling. Physics equipment!

So, that's what that intriguing collection of things was called!

Her father then opened the cabinet and allowed Marie to touch everything!

He explained to her that the rocks were samples of minerals, that the marvelous pink rock was quartz, that the mysterious objects were electroscopes, and that the small tubes were test tubes.

Her father, who was a professor of physics, also told her that every scientific theory had to be tested with experiments.

The next day, Marie's mother noticed a small green
spot on the tip of Marie's tongue.

What could it be? A strange disease? Her mother was
frightened at first. But the mystery soon unfolded.

In tears, Marie confessed to having tasted green ink with
the tip of her tongue!

Her mother yelled at her and then made her drink a glass
of milk.

Later that day, Marie's father questioned her about the green ink. He asked her why she had done such a stupid thing. Marie answered that she had tasted the green ink to "test" what she already knew. Green was a color common to many things: spinach, peas, parsley, mint candies. But she wasn't sure if all green things tasted the same.

Her father exclaimed: "Ah! Ah!" Then he turned to the mother and said: "I think Manyusia performed a small scientific experiment today!"

Each evening, shortly before going to bed, the children could join their parents in the living room.

They could leaf through illustrated books or play quiet games. Father read or talked with Mother.

Mother read at times, played the piano at others, but more often than not made shoes for the children. For Marie's mother no work was unworthy, and so she had learned how to use the shoemaker's sewing needle and cutting knife.

The children would listen to the sounds of their mother's hammer as it banged small golden nails into the soles. These sounds formed a lovely message.

One evening, the last day of a long vacation, Father told the children not to leaf through the illustrated books, and not to play. The children were supposed to read school books that evening, especially Bronya who was a very poor reader.

Father had cut out an alphabet of large letters from a cardboard box. But Bronya was not making any progress.

She sat on the carpet with an open book on her knees. She started to read out loud, hesitantly, pointing to the letters and stumbling on each word.

Then, all of a sudden, Marie, who was sitting near Bronya, impatiently pulled the book from Bronya's hands and promptly read the entire page. Then she turned the page to continue!

At that point Marie became aware of the stillness in the room. She felt that all eyes were upon her.

"I'm sorry! Forgive me!" she shouted. "I didn't do it on purpose!" And suddenly she started to cry.

"I've always helped Bronya put away her alphabet cards into the box," she said through her tears, "and that's how I learned! It was so easy! Forgive me! Forgive me!"

Father and Mother tried to cheer her up, telling her that she had done nothing wrong. But both of them agreed that Marie was too small to be reading. She was only four years old. Her mind would get tired.

And, then, they did not want a child prodigy.

From that moment on, her father and mother kept an eye on Marie to stop her from reading. Her brothers and sisters were instructed to do the same. Marie was supposed to play.

Every so often, a scream would echo throughout the house: "Anciupecio is reading!" The book would then be snatched from Marie's hands, and she would be brought out to the garden to play.

But also from that moment on, Marie's parents would be implored continually by the small voice of a little girl who would ask: "May I read now? May I please read?"

Finally, the father came to the conclusion that the best thing for Marie was to go to school a little earlier. Her intelligence needed exercise.

Although she was the youngest at school, Marie was undoubtedly the cleverest.

In those days Marie's country, Poland, had been invaded by Russia. The conquerors forced the schools to teach Russian history and its students to read and speak Russian.

Every so often a very mean inspector, announced by the ring of a bell, would arrive to make sure that these things were being done.

But the teachers would secretly tell the children the history of their own unfortunate nation. This confused the children. All those dates and names to remember!

When the bell signaled the inspector's arrival, it was Marie who would save the situation, by quoting the famous Russian names and dates without error or hesitation.

The inspector would go away satisfied. But afterward, little Marie, being sensitive and emotional, would cry desperately.

As time went by, Marie learned not to cry for every little thing. But her love of learning, especially of scientific subjects, never changed.

Like a dream, her father's marvelous physics equipment always floated around in her mind.

And so Marie went on to study physics, becoming a great scientist. With her husband, Pierre Curie, she discovered a new strange element—radium—which would constantly emit rays, heat, and a delicate mysterious blue light. This was one of the great scientific discoveries of the twentieth century.

All inquires should be addressed to:
Barron's Educational Series, Inc.
250 Wireless Boulevard
Hauppauge, NY 11788

Library of Congress Catalog Card No. 92–38955

International Standard Book No. 0-8120-6340-6 (hardcover)
0-8120-1558-4 (paperback)

CIP
92–38955